BIG
BEASTS
Whale

Stephanie Turnbull

Published by Smart Apple Media
P.O. Box 1329
Mankato, MN 56002

Printed in the United States of America,
at Corporate Graphics in North Mankato, Minnesota.

Designed by Helen James
Edited by Mary-Jane Wilkins

Library of Congress Cataloging-in-Publication Data

Turnbull, Stephanie.
  Whale / Steph Turnbull.
    p. cm. -- (Big beasts)
  Includes index.
  Summary: "An introduction on whales, the big beasts in the ocean.
Describes how whales swim, find food, communicate, and care for
their young. Also mentions the different kinds of whales and their
differences"--Provided by publisher.
  ISBN 978-1-59920-838-1 (hardcover, library bound)
  1. Whales--Juvenile literature. I. Title.
  QL737.C4T87 2013
  599.5--dc23
                          2012004117

Photo acknowledgements
l = left, r = right; t = top, b = bottom, c = center
page 1 Josef78/Shutterstock; 3 Karel Gallas/Shutterstock;
4 Sebastien Burel/Shutterstock; 5 Four Oaks/Eric Isselée/
Shutterstock; 6 Christian Darkin/Shutterstock; 7b Hemera/
Thinkstock, t iStockphoto/Thinkstock; 8-9 Catmando/
Shutterstock; 10 iStockphoto/Thinkstock; 11 Richard Fitzer/
Shutterstock; 12 jo Crebbin/Shutterstock; 13 Hemera/Thinkstock,
c Dorling Kindersley RF/Thinkstock; 14 Zap Ichigo/Shutterstock;
15 Hemera/Thinkstock; 16 Xavier MARCHANT/Shutterstock;
17 iStockphoto/Thinkstock; 18-19 Christopher Meder-
Photography/Shutterstock; 20 iStockphoto/Thinkstock;
21t Dorling Kindersley RF/Thinkstock; b Viacheslav V. Fedorov/
Shutterstock; 22t Dorling Kindersley RF/Thinkstock, b Christian
Darkin/Shutterstock; 23t alexsvirid, b dny3d/both Shutterstock
Cover Tom Middleton/Shutterstock

DAD0503
042012
9 8 7 6 5 4 3 2 1

Contents

Whales are

gigantic!

King of the Ocean

Blue whales are the biggest animals in the world.

Fat called blubber keeps them warm and gives them energy.

They can weigh more than 38 big elephants.

Lots of Whales

There are many types of whales.
They live in oceans all over the world.

Right whales are friendly giants
who often swim near boats.

Beluga whales have a squishy lump on their head called a melon.

Killer whales sometimes attack other whales.

Strong Swimmers

Whales are sleek and smooth for zipping through water.

They have flat flippers and a strong tail that powers up and down, not side to side like a fish.

Whales can swim a **long** way.

Blowholes

Whales breathe air, like we do.
They have nostrils called blowholes.

Some whales have one
blowhole. Others have two.

They blast
out air with
a whoooosh!

Then they
breathe in
and dive back
underwater.

11

Open Wide!

Many whales have long bristles called baleen hanging from their top jaw.

They take huge mouthfuls of water, then push it out through the baleen. Tiny shrimps called krill are left behind and swallowed.

Whales eat millions of krill every day.

Toothy Killers

Some whales
have sharp
teeth instead
of baleen.

They hunt in groups,
searching for fish, squid,
or even seals to gobble up.

Sometimes they slam into
their prey first to stun it.

Amazing Acrobats

Whales are so powerful that they can leap right out of the water!

They do this to show off and to get rid of creatures on their skin.

Big Babies

Whale babies
are called calves.

Females have one calf every few years.

Calves stay close to their mom.
They drink her milk, which is thick
like toothpaste to stop it floating away.

Whale Talk

Whales call to each other by passing air through hollow spaces in their heads.

WheeeeEEEE ....

Muuuuuurrrr......

Humpback whales sing beautiful songs using whistles and moans.

Oooooo...

Sperm whales make echoing clicks.

Click
clack
click

EEEE!

CRAAAAK!

SQUAWK!

BRRRR!

Beluga whales squeak, squeal, and squawk.

21

BIG Facts

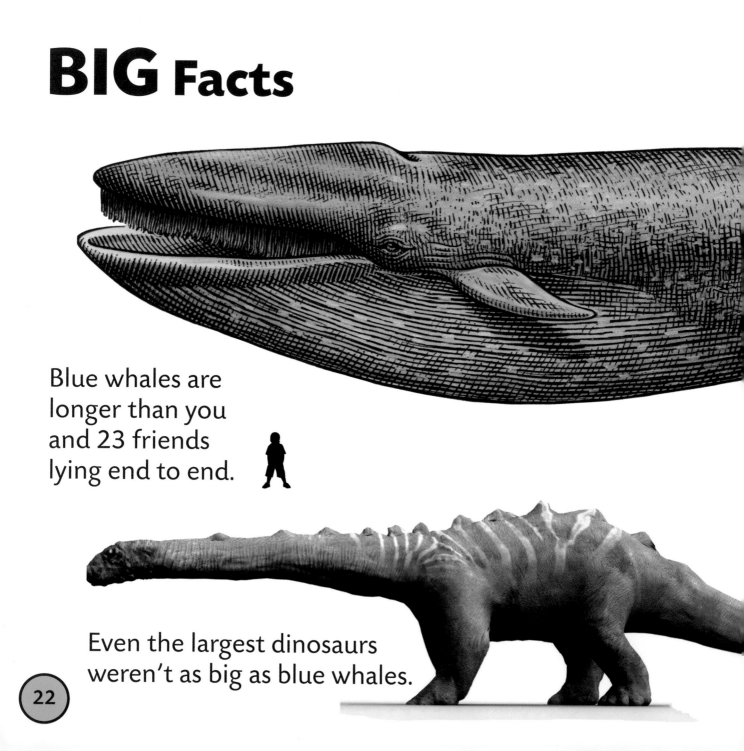

Blue whales are longer than you and 23 friends lying end to end.

Even the largest dinosaurs weren't as big as blue whales.

Newborn blue whale babies weigh the same as adult hippos.

When a big whale breathes out, its spout of air and spray shoots higher than a house.

23

Useful Words

baleen
Long bristles like combs in a whale's mouth. Blue whales, humpbacks, and some other whales have baleen.

blowhole
A whale's nostril on top of its head. It shuts when the whale is underwater.

prey
An animal that is hunted by another animal.

Index

Web Link
This website has whale facts, quizzes, and pictures to print: www.enchantedlearning.com/subjects/whales